# THE HOBBIT™

## THE DESOLATION OF SMAUG

### The Movie Storybook

First U.S. edition

First published by HarperCollins *Children's Books* in 2013.

Text by Paddy Kempshall

Adapted from the screenplay by Fran Walsh, Philippa Boyens and Peter Jackson
Edited by Neil Dunnicliffe, Design by Wayne Redwood, Production by Sian Smith

For information about permission to reproduce selections from this book,
write to Permissions, Houghton Mifflin Harcourt Publishing Company,
215 Park Avenue South, New York, New York 10003.

*The Hobbit: The Desolation of Smaug The Movie Storybook* is a companion to the film *The Hobbit: The Desolation of Smaug*
and is published with the permission, but not the approval, of the Estate of the late J.R.R. Tolkien.
Dialogue quotations are from the film, not the novel.

*The Hobbit* is published in the United States by Houghton Mifflin Harcourt.

*Library of Congress Cataloging-in-Publication Data is available.*
ISBN 978-0-547-90198-5

Printed and bound in Spain
HC 10 9 8 7 6 5 4 3 2 1

# THE HOBBIT™

## THE DESOLATION OF SMAUG

## The Movie Storybook

Houghton Mifflin Harcourt
Boston   New York
2013

For a hobbit from Hobbiton fond of his comfortable life, Bilbo Baggins is on a dangerous adventure. When the Wizard Gandalf and 13 Dwarves, led by Thorin Oakenshield, appear on Bilbo's doorstep, they persuade him to travel with them to the Lonely Mountain, far in the east. Their quest is to defeat the Dragon, Smaug and help reclaim the lost Dwarf Kingdom of Erebor.

During their journey, Bilbo has almost been a Troll's dinner, been saved by Giant Eagles and found a magic Ring that can turn him invisible.

Now, midway through their Quest, Bilbo and the Company of Dwarves are running out of time. They have to reach the Lonely Mountain before the last light of Durin's Day shines upon a special door, revealing the secret entrance into Smaug's lair.

But these lands are dangerous and the Company must escape a vicious pack of Wargs and Orcs who are chasing them.

They need to find somewhere to hide as soon as they can.

Gandalf tells them about a house nearby where they might be able to seek shelter. The only problem is, the person who lives there might also kill them!

Bilbo and his friends have no choice, so they follow Gandalf to a large hedge with a gate in it. Behind the gate, they see a wooden cabin.

Suddenly, there is an ear-splitting roar behind them. Turning, Bilbo and the Company see a huge bear-like creature charging at them.

The Dwarves race for the door to the cabin – only to find it locked! With the vicious bear getting closer, they try forcefully to shove the door open, but it won't budge.

With the bear closing in, Thorin manages to lift the latch and Bilbo and the Dwarves tumble inside. They slam the door behind them and the bear crashes into it, shaking the cabin to its foundations.

Gandalf grimly explains that the strange creature is actually the owner of the dwelling. His name is Beorn and he is a skin-changer who is able to transform himself into a huge bear-like creature.

The following morning, the Company meet their host, Beorn. Accustomed to living alone with his beloved animals, he is not pleased to have guests in his home. But once he learns that the Orc Commander, Azog, is chasing the Dwarves, he becomes more at ease. Beorn hates Orcs, and Azog most especially.

Gandalf learns from Beorn that there are other dangers lurking ahead. An evil Necromancer now inhabits the old fortress of Dol Guldur that lies deep within the forest of Mirkwood.

But at the edge of the forest, Gandalf receives a dark warning. He realises that he must leave the Company to venture on without him. It is his task to discover, once and for all, the true identity of the Necromancer.

Before leaving the Company on their own, he warns them not to stray from the Elven Road.

Mirkwood Forest is gloomy and dank. The Company immediately feel cold and afraid. All around them are overgrown, rotten trees and vegetation that block out the light from above.

Along the narrow path into the woods, they can hear a strange noise, like a group of voices whispering all at once.

The path becomes darker and covered in sticky webs. Unbeknownst to the Company, they have strayed from the safety of the Elven Road!

The Company becomes lost amidst the darkness of Mirkwood.

Bilbo volunteers to climb the tallest tree to look for a path out of the woods. From the top, he can see the vast forest and spies a way out – they are saved. Or so he thinks. . .

While Bilbo enjoys the bright sunlight above the trees, he calls down to the others, but gets no answer! His feet have been wrapped in a sticky web. Before he can do anything, he stumbles and falls. When he lands, he sees a mass of giant spiders scuttling out of the trees, ready to sting him and his fellow travellers.

The spiders wrap Bilbo and the Dwarves in their strange webs and carry them away. Fortunately, Bilbo is carrying his sword and cuts himself out of the sticky, strong threads. He puts on his Ring and becomes invisible to the stalking predators.

To distract the spiders, Bilbo hurls a stick into the trees. All but one of the spiders is fooled. A large, fat spider stays behind. It prepares to eat Bombur and the other Dwarves!

Calling on courage that he never even knew he had, the tiny hobbit fights bravely and manages to slay the giant foe.

Quickly and quietly, he cuts his friends free.

While Bilbo is busy fighting, the Dwarves are under attack from more giant spiders.

Just when it appears all is lost, a tall and lithe Woodland Elf named Legolas emerges from out of the trees. He and his guards slay the last of the spiders.

However, this is no rescue. Instead Thorin and the other Dwarves are taken prisoner and led to the palace of Thranduil, the powerful Elf-Lord and King of the Woodland Realm.

Thorin is dragged before the King himself to be questioned, while the rest of the Company is thrown into the dungeons. Thranduil guesses that Thorin is on a quest to take back his kingdom and its treasure. He offers to release the Dwarves if they will agree to his terms.

Thorin refuses. Thranduil orders his guards to put him into the cells with the rest of the Company.

Meanwhile, Bilbo uses his magic Ring to follow his friends to the Elf King's palace. While the Elves are busy drinking and celebrating, Bilbo steals the keys to the Dwarves' cells.

Quickly freeing them, he takes them to the cellars above a racing river and bundles them into a stack of empty barrels! Bilbo pulls a lever, the floor opens up and they fall into the water below.

When the Elves realise that the Dwarves have escaped, they burst into the room just in time to see Bilbo disappear into the hole. Thranduil is furious.

The Elves quickly close the gates on the river and suddenly the Dwarves are trapped! As they desperately try to open the gates, a group of Orcs who had followed them through the forest spring to the attack!

Things are looking grim when Tauriel, the head of the Elven Guard, Legolas and a band of Elves join the battle. Amidst the confusion, the Dwarves open the gates and slip away.

Floating downstream, the Company finally land on a deserted shore. But they soon realise they are not alone. A stranger with a deadly bow appears out of the forest…

The man is called Bard, and the Dwarves tell him that they are merchants. Eventually they manage to persuade Bard that they will pay him well if he takes them to Lake-town and gives them new supplies and weapons.

Elsewhere, Gandalf meets Radagast at the tombs in the High Fells and together they discover that an old enemy is at work! To investigate this evil, he and Radagast head south for Dol Guldur.

Back at Lake-town, Bard manages to smuggle the Dwarves past the guards and into his own house. That night, Balin tells an old tale of when Smaug first came to Erebor and was injured by a fabled Black Arrow shot from a huge Dwarven weapon.

Time is passing quickly. The Dwarves only have two more days to reach the top of the Lonely Mountain. But for the time being, they are trapped in Bard's house with spies watching their every move!

Meanwhile, Bard discovers that the Dwarves aren't merchants after all, but are actually from Erebor and are trying to reclaim their kingdom.

When he returns to his house, he finds the Dwarves have crept out, under the cover of night, intent on reaching the Mountain.

The Dwarves are about to escape Lake-town, when they are captured by the Town's Guard.

They are dragged to the town square as prisoners and presented to the Master of Lake-town, the man who controls the city and its people. Thorin convinces the Master to let them go in return for a share of Smaug's treasure.

Far to the south, Gandalf and Radagast have arrived at Dol Guldur. Giving his friend a message to take back, Gandalf makes Radagast promise not to follow him and goes into the ruins alone.

Released at last, the Company travels from Lake-town until they spy a city in the distance –
the ruined city of Dale.

Bilbo and the Dwarves are desperate to find the special door that will open a secret entrance into the Lonely Mountain. They spot a Dwarven statue and discover that inside it is a hidden staircase that leads to the door.

When they reach the top of the Lonely Mountain, the sun is setting and time is running out. No one can find the keyhole in the secret entrance. As the last rays of sun die, Thorin tosses away his key in frustration… they have failed.

Unwilling to accept defeat, Bilbo sees the moon rise and has an idea. The 'last light' of Durin's Day is the light from the moon, not the sun! He quickly finds Thorin's key and opens the door.

Now, all he has to do is creep inside the cavern and steal a special white jewel, the legendary Arkenstone, from a fire-breathing Dragon!

Creeping into the darkness below, Bilbo finds himself amazed by the huge piles of gold and treasure stacked everywhere. As he scrambles over the coins and trinkets looking for the Arkenstone, he causes a landslide – revealing the bulbous, lidded eye of a huge sleeping Dragon!

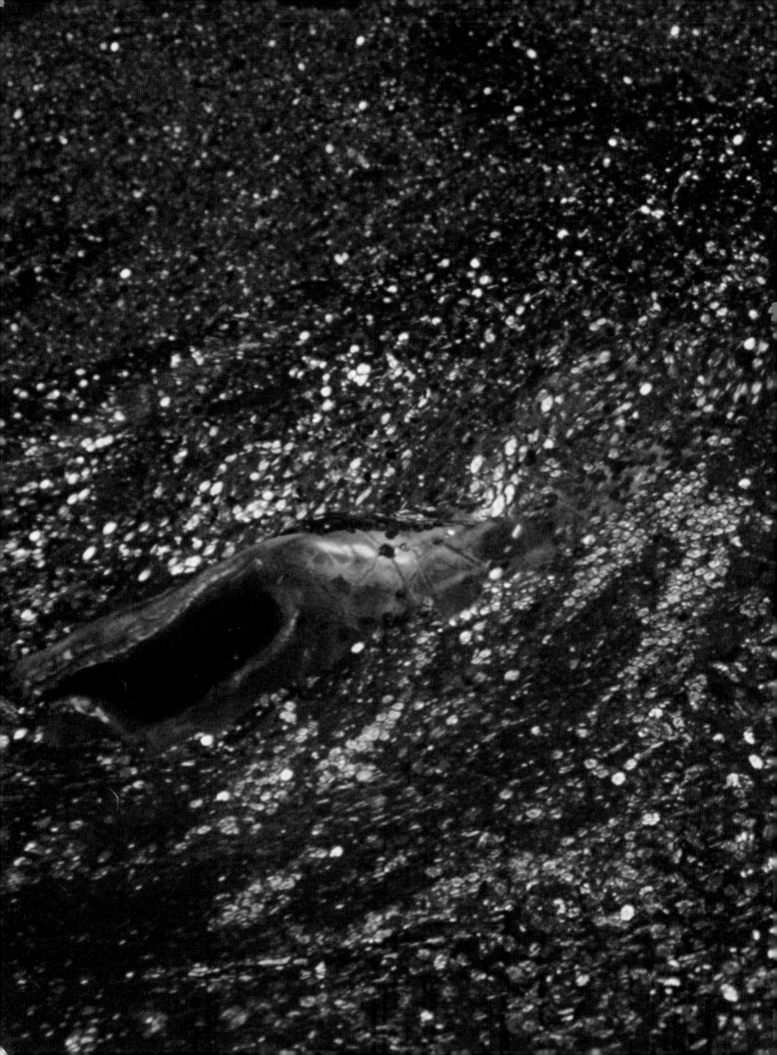

Too frightened to move, Bilbo reaches into his pocket and pulls out the Ring. Before he has time to put it on his finger and become invisible, the massive eyelid opens wide and the evil light of Smaug's giant red eye sweeps across the chamber towards the tiny hobbit. . .